St. John the Evangelist

Gospel Writer & Apostle

Prayer Journal

"The Disciple whom Jesus Loved"

Feast Day
27 December

Back Cover Photo Source: Wikimedia Commons user Andreas F. Borchert
Used under the Creative Commons Attribution-Share Alike 4.0 International license.

ISBN 978-1-71665-704-7
©2020 Catholic Treehouse

"S. Gregory concludes with the following golden words (Hom. 15 in Ezech.): 'Do we seek to have our hearts inflamed with the fire of love? Then let us ponder over the words of S. John, for everything that he says is filled with the fire of love.' He breathes, repeats and enforces nothing else but the love of God, of Christ, and of our neighbor. He is like old men and lovers, who think and speak of nothing else but what they love and have loved all their lives."

THE GREAT BIBLICAL COMMENTARY OF CORNELIUS À LAPIDE

St. John the Evangelist
by Vladimir Borovikovsky

Biography of St. John the Evangelist

New Testament Accounts

John was the son of Zebedee and Salome, and the brother of James the Greater. In the Gospels the two brothers are often called after their father "the sons of Zebedee" and received from Christ the honorable title of *Boanerges*, i.e. "sons of thunder" (Mark 3:17). Originally they were fishermen and fished with their father in the Sea of Galilee. According to the usual and entirely probable explanation they became, however, for a time disciples of John the Baptist, and were called by Christ from the circle of John's followers, together with Peter and Andrew, to become His disciples (John 1:35-42). The first disciples returned with their new Master from the Jordan to Galilee and apparently both John and the others remained for some time with Jesus (cf. John ii, 12, 22; iv, 2, 8, 27 sqq.). Yet after the second return from Judea, John and his companions went back again to their trade of fishing until he and they were called by Christ to definitive discipleship (Matthew 4:18-22; Mark 1:16-20). In the lists of the Apostles John has the second place (Acts 1:13), the third (Mark 3:17), and the fourth (Matthew 10:3; Luke 6:14), yet always after James with the exception of a few passages (Luke 8:51; 9:28 in the Greek text; Acts 1:13).

From James being thus placed first, the conclusion is drawn that John was the younger of the two brothers. In any case John had a prominent position in the Apostolic body. Peter, James, and he were the only witnesses of the raising of Jairus's daughter (Mark 5:37), of the Transfiguration (Matthew 17:1), and of the Agony in Gethsemane (Matthew 26:37). Only he and Peter were sent into the city to make the preparation for the Last Supper (Luke 22:8). At the Supper itself his place was next to Christ on Whose breast he leaned (John 13:23, 25). According to the general interpretation John was also that "other disciple" who with Peter followed Christ after the arrest into the palace of the high-priest (John 18:15). John alone remained near his beloved Master at the foot of the Cross on Calvary with the Mother of Jesus and the pious women, and took the desolate Mother into his care as the last legacy of Christ (John 19:25-27). After the Resurrection John with Peter was the first of the disciples to hasten to the grave and he was the first to believe that Christ had truly risen (John 20:2-10). When later Christ appeared at the Sea of Galilee John was also the first of the seven disciples present who recognized his Master standing on the shore (John 21:7). The Fourth Evangelist has shown us most clearly how close the relationship was in which he always stood to his Lord and Master by the title with which he is accustomed to indicate himself without giving his name: "the disciple whom Jesus loved". After Christ's Ascension and the

Descent of the Holy Spirit, John took, together with Peter, a prominent part in the founding and guidance of the Church. We see him in the company of Peter at the healing of the lame man in the Temple (Acts 3:1 sqq.). With Peter he is also thrown into prison (Acts 4:3). Again, we find him with the prince of the Apostles visiting the newly converted in Samaria (Acts 8:14).

We have no positive information concerning the duration of this activity in Palestine. Apparently John in common with the other Apostles remained some twelve years in this first field of labor, until the persecution of Herod Agrippa I led to the scattering of the Apostles through the various provinces of the Roman Empire (cf. Acts 12:1-17). Notwithstanding the opinion to the contrary of many writers, it does not appear improbable that John then went for the first time to Asia Minor and exercised his Apostolic office in various provinces there. In any case a Christian community was already in existence at Ephesus before Paul's first labors there (cf. "the brethren", Acts 18:27, in addition to Priscilla and Aquila), and it is easy to connect a sojourn of John in these provinces with the fact that the Holy Ghost did not permit the Apostle Paul on his second missionary journey to proclaim the Gospel in Asia, Mysia, and Bithynia (Acts 16:6 sq.). There is just as little against such an acceptation in the later account in Acts of St. Paul's third missionary journey. But in any case such a sojourn by John in Asia in this first period was neither long nor uninterrupted. He returned with the other disciples to Jerusalem for the Apostolic Council (about A.D. 51). St. Paul in opposing his enemies in Galatia names John explicitly along with Peter and James the Less as a "pillar of the Church", and refers to the recognition which his Apostolic preaching of a Gospel free from the law received from these three, the most prominent men of the old Mother-Church at Jerusalem (Galatians 2:9). When Paul came again to Jerusalem after the second and after the third journey (Acts 18:22; 21:17 sq.) he seems no longer to have met John there. Some wish to draw the conclusion from this that John left Palestine between the years 52 and 55.

Of the other New-Testament writings, it is only from the three Epistles of John and the Apocalypse that anything further is learned concerning the person of the Apostle. We may be permitted here to take as proven the unity of the author of these three writings handed down under the name of John and his identity with the Evangelist. Both the Epistles and the Apocalypse, however, presuppose that their author John belonged to the multitude of personal eyewitnesses of the life and work of Christ (cf. especially 1 John 1:1-5; 4:14), that he had lived for a long time in Asia Minor, was thoroughly acquainted with the conditions existing in the various Christian communities there, and that he had a position of authority recognized by all Christian communities as leader of this part of the Church. Moreover, the Apocalypse tells us that its author was on the island of Patmos "for the word of God and for the testimony of Jesus", when he was honored with the heavenly Revelation contained in the Apocalypse (Revelation 1:9).

The alleged presbyter John

The author of the Second and Third Epistles of John designates himself in the superscription of each by the name *(ho presbyteros)*, "the ancient", "the old". Papias, Bishop of Hierapolis, also uses the same name to designate the "Presbyter John" as in addition to Aristion, his particular authority, directly after he has named the presbyters Andrew, Peter, Philip, Thomas, James, John, and Matthew (in Eusebius, *Church History III.*39.4). Eusebius was the first to draw, on account of these words of Papias, the distinction between a Presbyter John and the Apostle John, and this distinction was also spread in Western Europe by St. Jerome on the authority of Eusebius. The opinion of Eusebius has been frequently revived by modern writers, chiefly to support the denial of the Apostolic origin of the Fourth Gospel. The distinction, however, has no historical basis. First, the testimony of Eusebius in this matter is not worthy of belief. He contradicts himself, as in his "Chronicle" he expressly calls the Apostle John the teacher of Papias ("ad annum Abrah 2114"), as does Jerome also in Ep. lxxv, "Ad Theodoram", iii, and in *Illustrious Men* 18. Eusebius was also influenced by his erroneous doctrinal opinions as he denied the Apostolic origin of the Apocalypse and ascribed this writing to an author differing from St. John but of the same name. St. Irenaeus also positively designates the Apostle and Evangelist John as the teacher of Papias, and neither he nor any other writer before Eusebius had any idea of a second John in Asia (*Against Heresies* V.33.4). In what Papias himself says the connection plainly shows that in this passage by the word *presbyters* only Apostles can be understood. If John is mentioned twice the explanation lies in the peculiar relationship in which Papias stood to this, his most eminent teacher. By inquiring of others he had learned some things indirectly from John, just as he had from the other Apostles referred to. In addition he had received information concerning the teachings and acts of Jesus directly, without the intervention of others, from the still living "Presbyter John", as he also had from Aristion. Thus the teaching of Papias casts absolutely no doubt upon what the New-Testament writings presuppose and expressly mention concerning the residence of the Evangelist John in Asia.

The later accounts of John

The Christian writers of the second and third centuries testify to us as a tradition universally recognized and doubted by no one that the Apostle and Evangelist John lived in Asia Minor in the last decades of the first century and from Ephesus had guided the Churches of that province. In his "Dialogue with Tryphon" (Chapter 81) St. Justin Martyr refers to "John, one of the Apostles of Christ" as a witness who had lived "with us", that is, at Ephesus. St. Irenaeus speaks in very many places of the Apostle John and his residence in Asia and expressly declares that he wrote his Gospel at Ephesus (*Against Heresies* III.1.1), and that he had lived there until the reign of Trajan (loc. cit., II, xxii, 5). With Eusebius (*Church History III.*13.1) and others we are obliged to place the Apostle's banishment to Patmos in the reign of the Emperor Domitian (81-96). Previous to this, according to Tertullian's testimony, John had been thrown into a cauldron of boiling oil before the Porta Latina at Rome without suffering injury. After Domitian's death the Apostle returned to Ephesus during the reign of Trajan, and at Ephesus he died about A.D. 100 at a great age. Tradition reports many beautiful traits of the last years of his life: that he refused to remain under the same roof with Cerinthus; his touching anxiety about a youth who had become a robber; his constantly repeated words of exhortation at the end of his life, "Little children, love one another". On the other hand the stories told in the apocryphal Acts of John, which appeared as early as the second century, are unhistorical invention.

Feasts of St. John

St. John is commemorated on 27 December, which he originally shared with St. James the Greater. At Rome the feast was reserved to St. John alone at an early date, though both names are found in the Carthage Calendar, the Hieronymian Martyrology, and the Gallican liturgical books. The "departure" or "assumption" of the Apostle is noted in the Menology of Constantinople and the Calendar of Naples (26 September), which seems to have been regarded as the date of his death. The feast of St. John before the Latin Gate, supposed to commemorate the dedication of the church near the Porta Latina, is first mentioned in the Sacramentary of Adrian I (772-95).

St. John in Christian art

Early Christian art usually represents St. John with an eagle, symbolizing the heights to which he rises in the first chapter of his Gospel. The chalice as symbolic of St. John, which, according to some authorities, was not adopted until the thirteenth century, is sometimes interpreted with reference to the Last Supper, again as connected with the legend according to which St. John was handed a cup of poisoned wine, from which, at his blessing, the poison rose in the shape of a serpent. Perhaps the most natural explanation is to be found in the words of Christ to John and James "My chalice indeed you shall drink" (Matthew 20:23).

Citation: Fonck, L. (1910). St. John the Evangelist. In *The Catholic Encyclopedia*. New York: Robert Appleton Company. Retrieved August 12, 2020 from New Advent: *http://www.newadvent.org/cathen/08492a.htm*

St. John, Apostle and Evangelist
by Father Francis Xavier Weninger, 1876

St. John, Apostle and Evangelist of Jesus Christ, a brother of St. James, and son of Zebedee and Salome, was born at Bethsaida, a town in Galilee. Christ, our Lord, called him and his brother James to follow Him, at the time when they were mending their nets in a boat on the shore of the Sea of Galilee. John, without delay, left all he possessed, even his own father, and, with his brother, followed the Lord. Although the youngest of the Apostles, he was beloved by the Savior above all the others; whence he is several times mentioned in the Gospel, as "the disciple whom Jesus loved." The cause of this special love of Jesus for him, was, according to the Holy Fathers, his virginal purity, which he kept undefiled, and the tender love he bore to the Lord. "He was more beloved than all the other Apostles," writes St. Thomas Aquinas, "on account of his purity." "For the same reason," says St. Anselm, "God revealed more mysteries to him than to the other Apostles. Justly," says he, "did Christ the Lord reveal the greatest mysteries to him, because he surpassed all in virginal purity."

It is evident from the Gospel that St. John was one of the most intimate of the friends of the Lord, and was, in consequence, sometimes admitted into Christ's presence, when, except Peter and James, no other Apostle was allowed to be near. Thus, he was with Christ when He healed the mother-in-law of Peter; when He raised the daughter of Jairus from the dead; and when He was transfigured on Mount Thabor. He also accompanied Christ when He suffered His agony in the Garden of Olives. The other two above-named Apostles shared these favors with John; but none was permitted to lean upon the Savior's bosom, at the last supper, save John; none was recommended as son to the divine Mother, but John. Only he, of all the Apostles, followed Christ to Mount Calvary, and remained there with Him until His death. To recompense this love, Christ gave him to His Mother as her son, when He said: "Behold thy Mother!" Christ, who had lived in virginal chastity, would trust His Virgin Mother to no one else but John, who himself lived in virginal purity. As St. Jerome says: "Christ, a virgin, recommended Mary, a virgin, to John, a virgin." No greater grace could John have asked of Christ; no more evident proof could he have received of His love. The most precious thing which the Lord possessed on earth, His holy Mother, He commended to His beloved disciple. He took him as brother, by giving Him as son to His mother. Who cannot see from all this that Christ loved and honored St. John above all others?

How deeply this beloved disciple must have suffered by seeing his Savior die so ignominious a death, is easily to be conceived; and St. Chrysostom hesitates not to call him, therefore, a manifold martyr. After Christ had died on the Cross, had been taken from it, and interred with all possible honors, St. John returned home with the divine Mother, who was now also his mother, and waited for the glorious resurrection of the Lord. When this had taken place, he participated in the many apparitions of the Lord, by which the disciples were comforted, and doubtless received again particular marks of love from the Savior. He afterwards assisted, with the divine Mother and the Apostles, and other disciples of Christ, at the wonderful Ascension of the Lord. With these, also, he received, after a ten days' preparation, the Holy Ghost, on the great festival of Pentecost. Soon after this, he and Peter had, before all others, the grace to suffer for Christ's sake. For when these two Apostles had, in the name of Christ, miraculously healed a poor cripple who was lying at the door of the temple of Jerusalem, and improved this opportunity to show to the assembled people that Jesus of Nazareth was the true Messiah, they were seized, at the instigation of the chief priests, and were cast into prison. On the following day, the priests came together, and John and Peter were called before them, and asked in whose name, and by what power they had healed the cripple. Peter and John answered fearlessly, that it had been done in the name of Jesus Christ. The high priest dared not do anything further to them, but, setting them free, prohibited them from preaching, in future, the name of Christ. The two holy Apostles, however, nothing daunted, said: "If it be just in the sight of God to hear you rather than God, judge ye: for we cannot but speak the things which we have seen and heard."

St. John remained for some time in Jerusalem after this, and, with the other Apostles, was zealous in his endeavors to convert the Jews. When the Apostles separated, to preach the gospel over all the world, Asia Minor was assigned to St. John. Going thither, he began with great zeal his apostolic functions, and, by the gift of miracles, he converted many thousands to the faith of Christ. The many bishoprics which he instituted in the principal cities sufficiently prove this. In the course of time, he went also to other countries, preaching everywhere, with equal success, the word of Christ. The Emperor Domitian, who, after the death of the Emperor Nero, again began to persecute the Christians, ordered his officers to apprehend John, and bring him to Rome. Hardly had the holy Apostle arrived there, when he was commanded by the Emperor to sacrifice to the gods. As the Saint refused this, and fearlessly confessed Christ, the Emperor had him most cruelly scourged, and afterwards cast into a large caldron, filled with boiling oil. The Saint signed himself and the caldron with the holy cross, and remained unharmed when he was cast into it. This gave him an opportunity to announce, with great energy, to the assembled people, the gospel of Jesus Christ. The tyrant, who could not suffer this, had him taken out of the caldron, and sentenced him to banishment on the island of Patmos, to work in the mines, and perform other hard labor, in company with other Christians. St. John had, at that time, reached his ninetieth year, but was willing to undergo the unjust sentence.

After his arrival on the island, he had many and wonderful visions, which, by command of God, he put down in writing. The book which contains them is a part of Holy Writ, called the Apocalypse, or Revelation of St. John, a book which, according to St. Jerome, contains almost as many mysteries as words. After the death of Domitian, St. John was liberated, and returning to Ephesus, remained there until his death. He outlived all the other Apostles, as he reached the age of 100 years. His great labors, wearisome travels, and the many hardships he endured, at last enfeebled him to such an extent, that he could not go to the church without being carried. Frequently he repeated, in his exhortations, the words: "My little children, love one another." Some, annoyed at this, asked him why he so often repeated these words. He answered: "Because it is the commandment of the Lord; and if that is done, it suffices." By this he meant, that if we love each other rightly, we also love God; and when we love God and our neighbor, no more is needed to gain salvation; as love to God and to our neighbor contains the keeping of all other commandments.

The holy Apostle, who had suffered and labored so much for his beloved Master, was, at length, in the year 104, called by Him into heaven to receive his eternal reward. Besides the Apocalypse, to which we referred above, St. John also wrote three Epistles and his Gospel, on account of which he is called Evangelist. In his Gospel he gives many more facts than the other Evangelists, to prove the divinity of Jesus Christ; as, at that period, several heretics, as Cerinthus, Ebion, and the Nicolaites fought against this truth. In his Epistles, he exhorts particularly to love God and our neighbor, and to avoid heretics. In the first, among other things, he explains that love to God consists in keeping the commandments of God, which are not difficult to keep. "For this is the charity of God," writes he, "that we keep His commandments; and His commandments are not heavy." Of the love of our neighbor he says, that it must manifest itself in works, that is, we must assist our brethren in their need, and, if necessary, give even our lives for them, after the example of Christ. The holy Apostle exemplified his words by his actions.

Several holy fathers relate the following of him. The Saint had given a youth in charge of a bishop, with the commendation to instruct him carefully in virtue and sacred sciences. After some years, when the Saint returned to this bishop, and asked for the young man, he heard with deep sorrow that he had secretly left, and had joined the highwaymen, and had even become their chief. The holy Apostle set out at once, and went, not without danger to his life, into the woods, where the unhappy young man was said, to be. Finding him, he spoke most kindly to him, and succeeded in bringing him back. It is touching to read how the holy, man promised to atone for the youth's sins, if he would repent, and lead a better life. The youth followed the Saint's admonition, and did penance with such fervor and zeal that the Saint hesitated not to give him charge of the church at Ephesus.

PRACTICAL CONSIDERATIONS

I. Virginal chastity, which St. John preserved inviolate, was the principal reason why Christ the Lord loved him above all others, recommended him to His beloved mother, gave her to him as mother, and bestowed many other graces upon him. For nothing is more certain than what I have already more than once said to you; whoever preserves angelic purity, will have God as a friend and protector. But who will be the friend of him who is a slave to the vice of unchastity? Surely neither the Almighty, nor Angels, nor Saints; none but the unclean spirit; for he, as I told you only a few days ago, has the greatest pleasure in the vice of unchastity, which gains him more souls than all the other vices. Whose love and friendship do you seek? The love of Jesus Christ, or of the devil? Your lips tell me that you seek the friendship of the Lord, and not that of Satan. But your works — do they speak the same language? The boldness of your eyes, your tongue arid your manners, your frequent and frivolous associations with those of the other sex; and your equivocal or openly licentious speeches and songs, are surely no signs that you love chastity with your whole heart and endeavor to gain the love of Christ. Correct yourself in every point in which you need correction, or you can never expect to have Christ as your friend; neither can you hope to have the Mother of Jesus as your mother. She was given to the chaste John as a mother, and John, chaste and pure, was given to her as a son. If you would be a true child of Mary, if you wish Mary to be your mother, and to enjoy her motherly care and protection, as well during your life as in your dying hour, endeavor to live chaste according to your station, and avoid all that is against the purity required of you.

II. "My dear children, love one another." This was the admonition that St. John gave to the Christians. In his Epistles, he also commends nothing more earnestly than this. He teaches, however, that we must not only love with the tongue and in words, but in deed and in truth. Love to God must manifest itself in keeping the commandments of God, as he teaches in the following words: "For this is the charity of God, that we keep his commandments." (I John, v.) Those Who do not endeavor to keep them, must not say that they truly love God. Love to our neighbor must be made manifest by observing the words of Christ: " All things, therefore, whatsoever you would that men should do to you, do you also to them." (Matthew, vii.) "This sentence," says St. Paulinus, "we should have constantly before our eyes, and daily examine ourselves, if and how we have obeyed God's command." And it is this which I counsel you today to observe. For, you ought to know, that it is necessary for salvation, to love God and our neighbor with our whole heart; God, by keeping His commandments; our neighbor, by doing to him as we would wish that he should do to us. "Let nobody imagine that he will gain salvation by fasting, praying and other good works, who does not truly love God and his neighbor." Thus speaks St. Cyril of Alexandria.

The Gospel of St. John

Contents and scheme of the gospel

According to the traditional order, the Gospel of St. John occupies the last place among the four canonical Gospels. Although in many of the ancient copies this Gospel was, on account of the Apostolic dignity of the author inserted immediately after or even before the Gospel of St. Matthew, the position it occupies today was from the beginning the most usual and the most approved. As regards its contents, the Gospel of St. John is a narrative of the life of Jesus from His baptism to His Resurrection and His manifestation of Himself in the midst of His disciples. The chronicle falls naturally into four sections:

- *the prologue* (i, 1-18), containing what is in a sense a brief epitome of the whole Gospel in the doctrine of the Incarnation of the Eternal Word;
- *the first part* (i, 19-xii, 50), which recounts the public life of Jesus from His baptism to the eve of His Passion,
- *the second part* (xiii-xxi, 23), which relates the history of the Passion and Resurrection of the Savior;
- *a short epilogue* (xxi, 23-25), referring to the great mass of the Savior's words and works which are not recorded in the Gospel.

When we come to consider the arrangement of matter by the Evangelist, we find that it follows the historical order of events, as is evident from the above analysis. But the author displays in addition a special concern to determine exactly the time of the occurrence and the connection of the various events fitted into this chronological framework. This is apparent at the very beginning of his narrative when, as though in a diary he chronicles the circumstances attendant on the beginning of the Savior's public ministry, with four successive definite indications of the time (i, 29, 35, 43, ii, 1). He lays special emphasis on the first miracles: "This beginning of miracles did Jesus in Cana of Galilee" (ii, 11), and "This *is* again the second miracle that Jesus did, when he was come out of Judea into Galilee" (iv, 54). Finally, he refers repeatedly throughout to the great religious and national festivals of the Jews for the purpose of indicating the exact historical sequence of the facts related (ii, 13; v, 1; vi, 4; vii, 2; x, 22; xii, 1, xiii, 1).

All the early and the majority of modern exegetes are quite justified, therefore, in taking this strictly chronological arrangement of the events as the basis of their commentaries. The divergent views of a few modern scholars are without objective support either in the text of the Gospel or in the history of its exegesis.

Distinctive peculiarities

The Fourth Gospel is written in Greek, and even a superficial study of it is sufficient to reveal many peculiarities, which give the narrative a distinctive character. Especially characteristic is the vocabulary and diction. His vocabulary is, it is true, less rich in peculiar expressions than that of Paul or of Luke: he uses in all about ninety words not found in any other hagiographer. More numerous are the expressions which are used more frequently by John than by the other sacred writers. Moreover, in comparison with the other books of the New Testament, the narrative of St. John contains a very considerable portion of those words and expressions which might be called the common vocabulary of the Four Evangelists.

What is even more distinctive than the vocabulary is the grammatical use of particles, pronouns, prepositions, verbs, etc., in the Gospel of St. John. It is also distinguished by many peculiarities of style, — asyndeta, reduplications, repetitions, etc. On the whole, the Evangelist reveals a close intimacy with the Hellenistic speech of the first century of our era. which receives at his hands in certain expressions a Hebrew turn. His literary style is deservedly lauded for its noble, natural, and not inartistic simplicity. He combines in harmonious fashion the rustic speech of the Synoptics with the urban phraseology of St. Paul.

What first attracts our attention in the subject matter of the Gospel is the confinement of the narrative to the chronicling of events which took place in Judea and Jerusalem. Of the Savior's labors in Galilee John relates but a few events, without dwelling on details, and of these events only two — the multiplication of the loaves and fishes (vi, 1-16), and the sea-voyage (vi, 17-21) — are already related in the Synoptic Gospels.

A second limitation of material is seen in the selection of his subject-matter, for compared with the other Evangelists, John chronicles but few miracles and devotes his attention less to the works than to the discourses of Jesus. In most cases the events form, as it were, but a frame for the words, conversation, and teaching of the Savior and His disputations with His adversaries. In fact it is the controversies with the Sanhedrists at Jerusalem which seem especially to claim the attention of the Evangelist. On such occasions John's interest, both in the narration of the circumstances and in the recording of the discourses and conversation of the Savior, is a highly theological one. With justice, therefore, was John conceded even in the earliest ages of Christianity, the honorary title of the "theologian" of the Evangelists. There are, in particular, certain great truths, to which he constantly reverts in his Gospel and which may be regarded as his governing ideas, special mention should be made of such expressions as the Light of the World, the Truth, the Life, the Resurrection, etc. Not infrequently these or other phrases are found in pithy, gnomic form at the beginning of a colloquy or discourse of the Savior, and frequently recur, as a *leitmotif*, at intervals during the discourse (e.g. vi, 35, 48, 51, 58; x, 7, 9; xv, 1, 5; xvii, 1, 5; etc.).

In a far higher degree than in the Synoptics, the whole narrative of the Fourth Gospel centers round the Person of the Redeemer. From his very opening sentences John turns his gaze to the inmost recesses of eternity, to the Divine Word in the bosom of the Father. He never tires of portraying the dignity and glory of the Eternal Word Who vouchsafed to take up His abode among men that, while receiving the revelation of His Divine Majesty, we might also participate in the fullness of His grace and truth. As evidence of the Divinity of the Savior the author chronicles some of the great wonders by which Christ revealed His glory, but he is far more intent on leading us to a deeper understanding of Christ's Divinity and majesty by a consideration of His words, discourses, and teaching, and to impress upon our minds the far more glorious marvels of His Divine Love.

Authorship

If we except the heretics mentioned by Irenaeus (*Against Heresies* III.11.9) and Epiphanius (Haer., li, 3), the authenticity of the Fourth Gospel was scarcely ever seriously questioned until the end of the eighteenth century. Evanson (1792) and Bretschneider (1820) were the first to run counter to tradition in the question of the authorship, and, since David Friedrich Strauss (1834-40) adopted Bretschneider's views and the members of the Tübingen School, in the wake of Ferdinand Christian Baur, denied the authenticity of this Gospel, the majority of the critics outside the Catholic Church have denied that the Fourth Gospel was authentic. On the admission of many critics, their chief reason lies in the fact that John has too clearly and emphatically made the true Divinity of the Redeemer, in the strict metaphysical sense, the centre of his narrative. However, even Harnack has had to admit that, though denying the authenticity of the Fourth Gospel, he has sought in vain for any satisfactory solution of the Johannine problem: "Again and again have I attempted to solve the problem with various possible theories, but they led me into still greater difficulties, and even developed into contradictions." ("Gesch. der altchristl. Lit.", I, pt. ii, Leipzig, 1897, p. 678.)

A short examination of the arguments bearing on the solution of the problem of the authorship of the Fourth Gospel will enable the reader to form an independent judgment.

Direct historical proof

If, as is demanded by the character of the historical question, we first consult the historical testimony of the past, we discover the universally admitted fact that, from the eighteenth century back to at least the third, the Apostle John was accepted without question as the author of the Fourth Gospel. In the examination of evidence therefore, we may begin with the third century, and thence proceed back to the time of the Apostles.

The ancient manuscripts and translations of the Gospel constitute the first group of evidence. In the titles, tables of contents, signatures, which are usually added to the text of the separate Gospels, John is in every case and without the faintest indication of doubt named as the author of this Gospel. The earliest of the extant manuscripts, it is true, do not date back beyond the middle of the fourth century, but the perfect unanimity of all the codices proves to every critic that the prototypes of these manuscripts, at a much earlier date, must have contained the same indications of authorship. Similar is the testimony of the Gospel translations, of which the Syrian, Coptic, and Old Latin extend back in their earliest forms to the second century.

The evidence given by the early ecclesiastical authors, whose reference to questions of authorship is but incidental, agrees with that of the above mentioned sources. St. Dionysius of Alexandria (264-5), it is true, sought for a different author for the Apocalypse, owing to the special difficulties which were being then urged by the Millennarianists in Egypt; but he always took for granted as an undoubted fact that the Apostle John was the author of the Fourth Gospel. Equally clear is the testimony of Origen (d. 254). He knew from the tradition of the Church that John was the last of the Evangelists to compose his Gospel (Eusebius, *Church History* VI.25.6), and at least a great portion of his commentary on the Gospel of St. John, in which he everywhere makes clear his conviction of the Apostolic origin of the work has come down to us. Origen's teacher, Clement of Alexandria (d. before 215-6), relates as "the tradition of the old presbyters", that the Apostle John, the last of the Evangelists, "filled with the Holy Ghost, had written a spiritual Gospel" (Eusebius, op. cit., *VI*, xiv, 7).

Of still greater importance is the testimony of St. Irenaeus, Bishop of Lyons (d. about 202), linked immediately with the Apostolic Age as he is, through his teacher Polycarp, the disciple of the Apostle John. The native country of Irenaeus (Asia Minor) and the scene of his subsequent ministry (Gaul) render him a witness of the Faith in both the Eastern and the Western Church. He cites in his writings at least one hundred verses from the Fourth Gospel, often with the remark, "as John, the disciple of the Lord, says". In speaking of the composition of the Four Gospels, he says of the last: "Later John, the disciple of the Lord who rested on His breast, also wrote a Gospel, while he was residing at Ephesus in Asia". As here, so also in the other texts it is clear that by "John, the disciple of the Lord," he means none other than the Apostle John.

We find that the same conviction concerning the authorship of the Fourth Gospel is expressed at greater length in the Roman Church, about 170, by the writer of the Muratorian Fragment (lines 9-34). Bishop Theophilus of Antioch in Syria (before 181) also cites the beginning of the Fourth Gospel as the words of John. Finally, according to the testimony of a Vatican manuscript, Bishop Papias of Hierapolis in Phrygia, an immediate disciple of the Apostle John, included in his great exegetical work an account of the composition of the Gospel by St. John during which he had been employed as scribe by the Apostle.

It is scarcely necessary to repeat that, in the passages referred to, Papias and the other ancient writers have in mind but one John, namely the Apostle and Evangelist, and not some other Presbyter John, to be distinguished from the Apostle.

Indirect external evidence

In addition to the direct and express testimony, the first Christian centuries testify indirectly in various ways to the Johannine origin of the Fourth Gospel. Among this indirect evidence the most prominent place must be assigned to the numerous citations of texts from the Gospel which demonstrate its existence and the recognition of its claim to form a portion of the canonical writings of the New Testament, as early as the beginning of the second century. St. Ignatius of Antioch, who died under Trajan (98-117), reveals in the quotations, allusions, and theological views found in his Epistles, an intimate acquaintance with the Fourth Gospel. In the writings of the majority of the other Apostolic Fathers, also, a like acquaintance with this Gospel can scarcely be disputed, especially in the case of Polycarp, the "Martyrium of Polycarp", the "Epistle to Diognetus", and the "Pastor" of Hermas (cf. the list of quotations and allusions in F. X. Funk's edition of *The Apostolic Fathers*).

In speaking of St. Papias, Eusebius says (*Church History* III.39.17) that he used in his work passages from the First Epistle of St. John. But this Epistle necessarily presupposes the existence of the Gospel, of which it is in a way the introduction or companion work. Furthermore, St. Irenaeus cites a sentence of the "presbyters" which contains a quotation from John 14:2, and, according to the opinion of those entitled to speak as critics, St. Papias must be placed in the front rank of the presbyters.

Of the second-century apologists, St. Justin (d. about 166), in an especial manner, indicates by his doctrine of the Logos, and in many passages of his apologies the existence of the Fourth Gospel. His disciple Tatian, in the chronological scheme of his "Diatessaron", follows the order of the Fourth Gospel, the prologue of which he employs as the introduction to his work. In his "Apology" also he cites a text from the Gospel.

Like Tatian, who apostatized about 172 and joined the Gnostic sect of the Encratites, several other heretics of the second century also supply indirect testimony concerning the Fourth Gospel. Basilides appeals to John 1:8 and 2:4. Valentine seeks support for his theories of the ons in expressions taken from John; his pupil Heracleon composed, about 160, a commentary on the Fourth Gospel, while Ptolemy, another of his followers, gives an explanation of the prologue of the Evangelist. Marcion preserves a portion of the canonical text of the Gospel of St. John in his own apocryphal gospel. The Montanists deduce their doctrine of the Paraclete mainly from John 15 and 16. Similarly in his "True Discourse" (about 178) the pagan philosopher Celsus bases some of his statements on passages of the Fourth Gospel.

On the other hand, indirect testimony concerning this Gospel is also supplied by the oldest ecclesiastical liturgies and the monuments of early Christian art. As to the former, we find from the very beginning texts from the Fourth Gospel used in all parts of the Church, and not infrequently with special predilection. Again, to take one example, the raising of Lazarus depicted in the Catacombs forms, as it were, a monumental commentary on the eleventh chapter of the Gospel of St. John.

THE TESTIMONY OF THE GOSPEL ITSELF
The Gospel itself also furnishes an entirely intelligible solution of the question of authorship.

(1) The general character of the work
In the first place from the general character of the work we are enabled to draw some inferences regarding its author. To judge from the language, the author was a Palestinian Jew, who was well acquainted with the Hellenic Greek of the upper classes. He also displays an accurate knowledge of the geographical and social conditions of Palestine even in his slightest incidental references. He must have enjoyed personal intercourse with the Savior and must even have belonged to the circle of his intimate friends. The very style of his chronicle shows the writer to have been an eyewitness of most of the events. Concerning the Apostles John and James the author shows a thoroughly characteristic reserve. He never mentions their names, although he gives those of most of the Apostles, and once only, and then quite incidentally, speaks of "the sons of Zebedee" (21:2). On several occasions, when treating of incidents in which the Apostle John was concerned, he seems intentionally to avoid mentioning his name (John 1:37-40; 18:15, 16; cf. 20:3-10). He speaks of John the precursor nine times without giving him the title of "the Baptist", as the other Evangelists invariably do to distinguish him from the Apostle. All these indications point clearly to the conclusion that the Apostle John must have been the author of the Fourth Gospel.

(2) The express testimony of the author
Still clearer grounds for this view are to be found in the express testimony of the author. Having mentioned in his account of the Crucifixion that the disciple whom Jesus loved stood beneath the Cross beside the mother of Jesus (John 19:26 sqq.), he

adds, after telling of the Death of Christ and the opening of His side, the solemn assurance: "And he that saw it hath given testimony; and his testimony is true. And he knoweth that he saith true: that you also may believe" (xix, 35). According to the admission of all John himself is the "disciple whom the Lord loved". His testimony is contained in the Gospel which for many consecutive years he has announced by word of mouth and which he now sets down in writing for the instruction of the faithful. He assures us, not merely that this testimony is true, but that he was a personal witness of its truth. In this manner he identifies himself with the disciple beloved of the Lord who alone could give such testimony from intimate knowledge. Similarly the author repeats this testimony at the end of his Gospel. After again referring to the disciple whom Jesus loved, he immediately adds the words: "This is that disciple who giveth testimony of these things, and hath written these things; and we know that his testimony is true" (John 21:24). As the next verse shows, his testimony refers not merely to the events just recorded but to the whole Gospel. It is more in accordance with the text and the general style of the Evangelist to regard these final words as the author's own composition, should we prefer, however, to regard this verse as the addition of the first reader and disciple of the Apostle, the text constitutes the earliest and most venerable evidence of the Johannine origin of the Fourth Gospel.

(3) Comparison of the Gospel to the Johannine epistles
Finally we can obtain evidence concerning the author from the Gospel itself, by comparing his work with the three Epistles, which have retained their place among the Catholic Epistles as the writings of the Apostle John. We may here take for granted as a fact admitted by the majority of the critics, that these Epistles are the work of the same writer, and that the author was identical with the author of the Gospel. In fact the arguments based on the unity of style and language, on the uniform Johannine teaching, on the testimony of Christian antiquity, render any reasonable doubt of the common authorship impossible. At the beginning of the Second and Third Epistles the author styles himself simply "the presbyter" — evidently the title of honor by which he was commonly known among the Christian community. On the other hand, in his First Epistle, he emphasizes repeatedly and with great earnestness the feet that he was an eyewitness of the facts concerning the life of Christ to which he (in his Gospel) had borne testimony among the Christians: "That which was from the beginning, which we have heard, which we have seen with our eyes, which we have looked upon and our hands have handled, of the word of life: for the life was manifested; and we have seen and do bear witness, and declare unto you the life eternal, which was with the Father, and hath appeared to us: that which we have seen and have heard, we declare unto you" (1 John 1:1-3; cf. 4:14). This "presbyter" who finds it sufficient to use such an honorary title without qualification as his proper name, and was likewise an eye- and earwitness of the incidents of the Savior's life, can be none other than the Presbyter John mentioned by Papias, who can in turn be none other than John the Apostle.

We can therefore, maintain with the utmost certainty that John the Apostle, the favorite disciple of Jesus, was really the author of the Fourth Gospel.

CIRCUMSTANCES OF THE COMPOSITION

Passing over the intimate circumstances with which early legend has clothed the composition of the Fourth Gospel, we shall discuss briefly the time and place of composition, and the first readers of the Gospel.

As to the date of its composition we possess no certain historical information. According to the general opinion, the Gospel is to be referred to the last decade of the first century, or to be still more precise, to 96 or one of the succeeding years. The grounds for this opinion are briefly as follows:

- the Fourth Gospel was composed after the three Synoptics;
- it was written after the death of Peter, since the last chapter - especially xxi, 18-19 presupposes the death of the Prince of the Apostles;
- it was also written after the destruction of Jerusalem and the Temple, for the Evangelist's references to the Jews (cf. particularly xi, 18; xviii, 1; xix, 41) seem to indicate that the end of the city and of the people as a nation is already come;
- the text of xxi, 23, appears to imply that John was already far advanced in years when he wrote the Gospel;
- those who denied the Divinity of Christ, the very point to which St. John devotes special attention throughout his Gospel, began to disseminate their heresy about the end of the first century;
- finally, we have direct evidence concerning the date of composition. The so-called "Monarchian Prologue" to the Fourth Gospel, which was probably written about the year 200 or a little later, says concerning the date of the appearance of the Gospel: "He [sc. the Apostle John] wrote this Gospel in the Province of Asia, after he had composed the Apocalypse on the Island of Patmos". The banishment of John to Patmos occurred in the last year of Domitian's reign (i.e. about 95). A few months before his death (18 September, 96), the emperor had discontinued the persecution of the Christians and recalled the exiles (Eusebius, *Church History III.*20.5-7). This evidence would therefore refer the composition of the Gospel to A.D. 96 or one of the years immediately following.

The place of composition was, according to the above-mentioned prologue, the province of Asia. Still more precise is the statement of St. Irenaeus, who tells us that John wrote his Gospel "at Ephesus in Asia" (*Against Heresies III.*1.2). All the other early references are in agreement with these statements.

The first readers of the Gospel were the Christians of the second and third generations in Asia Minor. There was no need of initiating them into the elements of the Faith; consequently John must have aimed rather at confirming against the attacks of its opponents the Faith handed down by their parents.

CRITICAL QUESTIONS CONCERNING THE TEXT
As regards the text of the Gospel, the critics take special exception to three passages, 5:3-4; 7:53-8:11; and 21.

JOHN 5:3-4
The fifth chapter tells of the cure of the paralytic at the pool of Bethsaida in Jerusalem. According to the Vulgate the text of the second part of verse three and verse four runs as follows: "...waiting for the moving of the water. And an angel of the Lord descended at certain times into the pond, and the water was moved. And he that went down first into the pond after the motion of the water, was made whole, of whatsoever infirmity he lay under." But these words are wanting in the three oldest manuscripts, the Codex Vaticanus (B), Codex Sinaiticus (aleph), and Codex Bez (D), in the original text of the palimpsest of St. Ephraem (C), in the Syrian translation of Cureton, as well as in the Coptic and Sahidic translations, in some minuscules, in three manuscripts of the Itala, in four of the Vulgate, and in some Armenian manuscripts. Other copies append to the words a critical sign which indicates a doubt as to their authenticity. The passage is therefore regarded by the majority of modern critics, including the Catholic exegetes, Schegg, Schanz, Belser, etc., as a later addition by Papias or some other disciple of the Apostle.

Other exegetes, e.g. Corluy, Comely, Knabenbauer, and Murillo, defend the authenticity of the passage urging in its favor important internal and external evidence. In the first place the words are found in the Codex Alexandrinus (A), the emended Codex Ephraemi (C), in almost all minuscule manuscripts, in six manuscripts of the Itala, in most of the codices of the Vulgate, including the best, in the Syrian Peshito, in the Syrian translation of Philoxenus (with a critical mark), in the Persian, Arabic, and Slavonic translations, and in some manuscripts of the Armenian text. More important is the fact that, even before the date of our present codices, the words were found by many of the Greek and Latin Fathers in the text of the Gospel. This is clear from Tertullian, Didymus of Alexandria, St. John Chrysostom, St. Cyril of Alexandria, St. Ambrose, St. Augustine, although the last-mentioned, in his tractate on the Gospel of St. John, omits the passage.

The context of the narrative seems necessarily to presuppose the presence of the words. The subsequent answer of the sick man (v. 7), "Sir, I have no man, when the water is troubled, to put me into the pond. For whilst I am coming, another goeth down before me", could scarcely be intelligible without verse 4, and the Evangelist is not accustomed to omit such necessary information from his text. Thus both sides have good grounds for their opinions, and no final decision on the question, from the standpoint of the textual critic, seems possible.

JOHN 7:53-8:11

This passage contains the story of the adulteress. The external critical evidence seems in this ease to give still clearer decision against the authenticity of this passage. It is wanting in the four earliest manuscripts (B, A, C, and *aleph*) and many others, while in many copies it is admitted only with the critical mark, indicative of doubtful authenticity. Nor is it found in the Syrian translation of Cureton, in the Sinaiticus, the Gothic translation, in most codices of the Peshito, or of the Coptic and Armenian translations, or finally in the oldest manuscripts of the Itala. None of the Greek Fathers have treated the incident in their commentaries, and, among Latin writers, Tertullian, Cyprian, and Hilary appear to have no knowledge of this pericope.

Notwithstanding the weight of the external evidence of these important authorities, it is possible to adduce still more important testimony in favor of the authenticity of the passage. As for the manuscripts, we know on the authority of St. Jerome that the incident "was contained in many Greek and Latin codices" (Contra Pelagium, II, xvii), a testimony supported today by the Codex Bez of Canterbury (D) and many others. The authenticity of the passage is also favored by the Vulgate, by the Ethiopians Arabic, and Slavonic translations, and by many manuscripts of the Itala and of the Armenian and Syrian text. Of the commentaries of the Greek Fathers, the books of Origen dealing with this portion of the Gospel are no longer extant; only a portion of the commentary of St. Cyril of Alexandria has reached us, while the homilies of St. John Chrysostom on the Fourth Gospel must be considered a treatment of selected passages rather than of the whole text. Among the Latin Fathers, Sts. Ambrose and Augustine included the pericope in their text, and seek an explanation of its omission from other manuscripts in the fact that the incident might easily give rise to offense (cf. especially Augustine, "De coniugiis adulteris", II, vii). It is thus much easier to explain the omission of the incident from many copies than the addition of such a passage in so many ancient versions in all parts of the Church. It is furthermore admitted by the critics that the style and mode of presentation have not the slightest trace of apocryphal origin, but reveal throughout the hand of a true master. Too much importance should not be attached to variations of vocabulary, which may be found on comparing this passage with the rest of the Gospel, since the correct reading of the text is in many places doubtful, and any such differences of language may be easily harmonized with the strongly individual style of the Evangelist.

It is thus possible, even from the purely critical standpoint, to adduce strong evidence in favor of the canonicity and inspired character of this pericope, which by decision of the Council of Trent, forms a part of the Holy Bible.

John 21

Concerning the last chapter of the Gospel a few remarks will suffice. The last two verses of the twentieth chapter indicate clearly indeed that the Evangelist intended to terminate his work here: "Many other signs also did Jesus in the sight of his disciples, which are not written in this book. But these are written, that you may believe that Jesus is the Christ, the Son of God: and that believing, you may have life in his name" (xx, 30 sq.). But the sole conclusion that can be deduced from this is that the twenty-first chapter was afterwards added and is therefore to be regarded as an appendix to the Gospel. Evidence has yet to be produced to show that it was not the Evangelist, but another, who wrote this appendix. The opinion is at present fairly general, even among critics, that the vocabulary, style, and the mode of presentation as a whole, together with the subject-matter of the passage reveal the common authorship of this chapter and the preceding portions of the Fourth Gospel.

Historical genuineness

Objections raised against the historical character of the Fourth Gospel

The historical genuineness of the Fourth Gospel is at the present time almost universally denied outside the Catholic Church. Since David Friedrich Strauss and Ferdinand Christian Baur this denial has been postulated in advance in most of the critical inquiries into the Gospels and the life of Jesus. Influenced by this prevailing tendency, Alfred Loisy also reached the point where he openly denied the historicity of the Fourth Gospel; in his opinion the author desired, not to write a history, but to clothe in symbolical garb his religious ideas and theological speculations.

The writings of Loisy and their rationalistic prototypes, especially those of the German critics, have influenced many later exegetes, who while wishing to maintain the Catholic standpoint in general, concede only a very limited measure of historical genuineness to the Fourth Gospel. Among this class are included those who acknowledge as historical the main outlines of the Evangelist's narrative, but see in many individual portions only symbolical embellishments. Others hold with H. J. Holtzmann that we must recognize in the Gospel a mixture of the subjective, theological speculations of the author and the objective, personal recollections of his intercourse with Christ, without any possibility of our distinguishing by sure criteria these different elements. That such a hypothesis precludes any further question as to the historical genuineness of the Johannine narrative, is evident, and is indeed candidly admitted by the representatives of these views.

On examining the grounds for this denial or limitation of the historical genuineness of John we find that they are drawn by the critics almost exclusively from the relation of the Fourth Gospel to the Synoptic narrative. On comparison three points of contrast are discovered: (1) with respect to the events which are related; (2) in regard to the mode of presentation; and (3) in the doctrine which is contained in the narrative.

(1) *The events related*

As regards the events related, the great contrast between John and the Synoptists in the choice and arrangement of materials is especially accentuated. The latter show us the Savior almost exclusively in Galilee, laboring among the common people: John, on the other hand, devotes himself chiefly to chronicling Christ's work in Judea, and His conflicts with the Sanhedrists at Jerusalem. An easy solution of this first difficulty is found in the special circumstances attending the composition of the Fourth Gospel. John may - in fact must - have assumed that the Synoptic narrative was known to his readers at the end of the first century. The interest and spiritual needs of these readers demanded primarily that he supplement the evangelical story in such a manner as to lead to a deeper knowledge of the Person and Divinity of the Savior, against which the first heresies of Cerinthus, the Ebionites, and the Nicolaites were being already disseminated in Christian communities. But it was chiefly in His discussions with the Scribes and Pharisees at Jerusalem that Christ had spoken of His Person and Divinity. In his Gospel, therefore John made it his primary purpose to set down the sublime teachings of Our Savior, to safeguard the Faith of the Christians against the attacks of the heretics. When we come to consider the individual events in the narrative, three points in particular are brought forward:

the duration of Christ's public ministry extends in the Fourth Gospel over at least two years, probably indeed over three years, and some months. However, the Synoptic account of the public life of Jesus can by no means be confined within the narrow space of one year, as some modern critics contend. The three earliest Evangelists also suppose the space of at least two years and some months.

The purification of the Temple is referred by John to the beginning of the Savior's ministry, while the Synoptists narrate it at the close. But it is by no means proven that this purification occurred but once. The critics bring forward not a single objective reason why we should not hold that the incident, under the circumstances related in the Synoptics, as well as those of the Fourth Gospel, had its historical place at the beginning and at the end of the public life of Jesus.

Notwithstanding all the objections brought forward, John is in agreement with the Synoptists as to the date of the Last Supper. It occurred on Thursday, the thirteenth day of Nisan, and the Crucifixion took place on Friday, the fourteenth. The fact that according to John, Christ held the Supper with His Apostles on Thursday, while, according to the Synoptists, the Jews ate the paschal lamb on Friday, is not irreconcilable with the above statement. The most probable solution of the question lies in the legitimate and widespread custom, according to which, when the fifteenth of Nisan fell on the Sabbath, as it did in the year of the Crucifixion, the paschal lamb was killed in the evening hours of the thirteenth of Nisan and the paschal feast celebrated on this or the following evening, to avoid all infringement of the strict sabbatic rest.

(2) The mode of presentation

As regards the mode of presentation, it is especially insisted that the great sublimity of the Fourth Gospel is difficult to reconcile with the homely simplicity of the Synoptics. This objection, however, entirely disregards the great differences in the circumstances under which the Gospels were written. For the Christians of the third generation in Asia living in the midst of flourishing schools, the Fourth Evangelist was forced to adopt an entirely different style from that employed by his predecessors in writing for the newly-converted Jews and pagans of the earlier period.

Another difficulty raised is the fact that the peculiar Johannine style is found not only in the narrative portions of the Gospel, but also in the discourses of Jesus and in the words of the Baptist and other personages. But we must remember that all the discourses and colloquies had to be translated from Aramaic into Greek, and in this process received from the author their distinctive unity of style. Besides in the Gospel, the intention is by no means to give a verbatim report of every sentence and expression of a discourse, a sermon, or a disputation. The leading ideas alone are set forth in exact accordance with the sense, and, in this manner, also, they come to reflect the style of the Evangelist. Finally, the disciple surely received from his Master many of the distinctive metaphors and expressions which imprint on the Gospel its peculiar character.

(3) The doctrinal content

The difference in doctrinal content lies only in the external forms and does not extend to the truths themselves. A satisfactory explanation of the dogmatic character of John's narrative, as compared with the stress laid on the moral side of the discourses of Jesus by the Synoptists, is to be found in the character of his first readers, to which reference has already been repeatedly made. To the same cause, also, must be ascribed the further difference between the Gospels namely, why John makes his teaching centre around the Person of Jesus, while the Synoptics bring into relief rather the Kingdom of God. At the end of the first century there was no need for the Evangelist to repeat the lessons concerning the Kingdom of Heaven, already amply treated by his predecessors.

His was the especial task to emphasize, in opposition to the heretics, the fundamental truth of the Divinity of the Founder of this Kingdom, and by chronicling those words and works of the Redeemer in which He Himself had revealed the majesty of His glory, to lead the faithful to a more profound knowledge of this truth.

It is superfluous to say that in the teaching itself, especially regarding the Person of the Redeemer, there is not the slightest contradiction between John and the Synoptists. The critics themselves have to admit that even in the Synoptic Gospels Christ, when He speaks of His relations with the Father, assumes the solemn "Johannine" mode of speech. It will be sufficient to recall the impressive words: "And no one knoweth the Son, but the Father: neither doth any one know the Father, but the Son, and he to whom it shall please the Son to reveal him" (Matthew 11:27; Luke 10:22).

(4) Positive Evidence for the Historical Genuineness of the Gospel
The reasons urged against the genuineness of the Fourth Gospel are devoid of all conclusive force. On the other hand, its genuineness is vouched for by the whole character of the narrative. From the very beginning the events are portrayed with the precision of an eyewitness; the most minute subsidiary circumstances are mentioned; not the least suggestion can be found that the author had any other object in mind than the chronicling of the strict historical truth. A perusal of the passages describing the call of the first disciples (i, 35-51), the Marriage at Cana (ii, 1-11), the conversation with the Samaritan woman (iv, 3-42), the healing of the man born blind (ix, 1-41), the raising of Lazarus (xi, 1-47), is sufficient to convince one that such a chronicle must necessarily lead the readers into error, if the events which are described be otherwise than true in the historical sense.

To this must be added the express assertion made repeatedly by the Evangelist that he speaks the truth and claims for his words unqualified belief (19:35; 20:30 sq.; 21:24; 1 John 1:1-4). To reject these assurances is to label the Evangelist a worthless impostor, and to make of his Gospel an unsolvable historical and psychological enigma.

And finally, the verdict of the entire Christian past has certainly a distinct claim to consideration in this question, since the Fourth Gospel has always been unhesitatingly accepted as one of the chief and historically credible sources of our knowledge of the life of Jesus Christ. With entire justice, therefore, have the contrary views been condemned in clauses 16-18 of the Decree "Lamentabili" (3 July, 1907) and in the Decree of the Biblical Commission of 29 May, 1907.

Object and importance

The intention of the Evangelist in composing the Gospel is expressed in the words which we have already quoted: "But these are written that you may believe that Jesus is the Christ, the Son of God" (xx, 31). He wished also by his work to confirm the faith of the disciples in the Messianic character and the Divinity of Christ. To attain his object, he selected principally those discourses and colloquies of Jesus in which the self-revelation of the Redeemer laid clearest emphasis on the Divine Majesty of His Being. In this manner John wished to secure the faithful against the temptations of the false learning by means of which the heretics might prejudice the purity of their faith. Towards the narrative of the earlier Evangelists John's attitude was that of one who sought to fill out the story of the words and works of the Savior, while endeavoring to secure certain incidents from misinterpretation. His Gospel thus forms a glorious conclusion of the joyous message of the Eternal Word. For all time it remains for the Church the most sublime testimony of her faith in the Son of God, the radiant lamp of truth for her doctrine, the never-ceasing source of loving zeal in her devotion to her Master, Who loves her even to the end.

Sources

Commentaries on the Gospel of St. John. In early Christian times: the Homilies of St. John Chrysostom and the Tractates of St. Augustine; the extant portions of the commentaries of Origen and St. Cyril of Alexandria; the expositions of Theophylactus and Euthymius, who generally follow Chrysostom, and the exegetical works of St. Bede, who follows Augustine. In the Middle Ages: the interpretations of St. Thomas Aquinas and St. Bonaventure, of Blessed Albertus Magnus, Rupert of Deutz, And St. Bruno Of Segni.

Citation: Fonck, L. (1910). Gospel of St. John. In *The Catholic Encyclopedia*. New York: Robert Appleton Company. Retrieved August 12, 2020 from New Advent: http://www.newadvent.org/cathen/08438a.htm

Dearly beloved, let us love one another: for charity is of God. And every one that loveth is born of God and knoweth God.

Biblical Novena to St. John the Evangelist

Day 1: Matthew 4:18–22

And Jesus walking by the Sea of Galilee, saw two brethren, Simon who is called Peter, and Andrew his brother, casting a net into the sea (for they were fishers). And he saith to them: Come ye after me, and I will make you to be fishers of men. And they immediately leaving their nets, followed him. And going on from thence, he saw other two brethren, James the son of Zebedee, and John his brother, in a ship with Zebedee their father, mending their nets: and he called them. And they forthwith left their nets and father, and followed him.

Day 2: Matthew 17:1–8

And after six days Jesus taketh unto him Peter and James, and John his brother, and bringeth them up into a high mountain apart: And he was transfigured before them. And his face did shine as the sun: and his garments became white as snow. And behold there appeared to them Moses and Elias talking with him. And Peter answering, said to Jesus: Lord, it is good for us to be here: if thou wilt, let us make here three tabernacles, one for thee, and one for Moses, and one for Elias. And as he was yet speaking, behold a bright cloud overshadowed them. And lo, a voice out of the cloud, saying: This is my beloved Son, in whom I am well pleased: hear ye him. And the disciples hearing, fell upon their face, and were very much afraid. And Jesus came and touched them: and said to them, Arise, and fear not. And they lifting up their eyes saw no one but only Jesus.

Day 3: Mark 6:7–13, 30–33

And he called the twelve; and began to send them two and two, and gave them power over unclean spirits. And he commanded them that they should take nothing for the way, but a staff only: no scrip, no bread, nor money in their purse, But to be shod with sandals, and that they should not put on two coats. And he said to them: Wheresoever you shall enter into an house, there abide till you depart from that place. And whosoever shall not receive you, nor hear you; going forth from thence, shake off the dust from your feet for a testimony to them. And going forth they preached that men should do penance: And they cast out many devils, and anointed with oil many that were sick, and healed them.... And the apostles coming together unto Jesus, related to him all things that they had done and taught. And he said to them: Come apart into a desert place, and rest a little. For there were many coming and going: and they had not so much as time to eat. And going up into a ship, they went into a desert place apart. And they saw them going away, and many knew: and they ran flocking thither on foot from all the cities, and were there before them.

Day 4: Mark 10:35–45

And James and John the sons of Zebedee, come to him, saying: Master, we desire that whatsoever we shall ask, thou wouldst do it for us: But he said to them: What would you that I should do for you? And they said: Grant to us, that we may sit, one on thy right hand, and the other on thy left hand, in thy glory. And Jesus said to them: You know not what you ask. Can you drink of the chalice that I drink of: or be baptized with the baptism wherewith I am baptized? But they said to him: We can. And Jesus saith to them: You shall indeed drink of the chalice that I drink of: and with the baptism wherewith I am baptized, you shall be baptized. But to sit on my right hand, or on my left, is not mine to give to you, but to them for whom it is prepared. And the ten hearing it, began to be much displeased at James and John. But Jesus calling them, saith to them: You know that they who seem to rule over the Gentiles, lord it over them: and their princes have power over them. But it is not so among you: but whosoever will be greater, shall be your minister. And whosoever will be first among you, shall be the servant of all. For the Son of man also is not come to be ministered unto, but to minister, and to give his life a redemption for many.

Day 5: Mark 14:32–33

And they came to a farm called Gethsemani. And he saith to his disciples: Sit you here, while I pray. And he taketh Peter and James and John with him; and he began to fear and to be heavy.

Day 6: Luke 8:50–51

And Jesus hearing this word, answered the father of the maid: Fear not; believe only, and she shall be safe. And when he was come to the house, he suffered not any man to go in with him, but Peter and James and John, and the father and mother of the maiden.

Day 7: Luke 9:51–56

And it came to pass, when the days of his assumption were accomplishing, that he steadfastly set his face to go to Jerusalem. And he sent messengers before his face; and going, they entered into a city of the Samaritans, to prepare for him. And they received him not, because his face was of one going to Jerusalem. And when his disciples James and John had seen this, they said: Lord, wilt thou that we command fire to come down from heaven, and consume them? And turning, he rebuked them, saying: You know not of what spirit you are. The Son of man came not to destroy souls, but to save. And they went into another town.

Day 8: John 19:25–27

Now there stood by the cross of Jesus, his mother, and his mother's sister, Mary of Cleophas, and Mary Magdalen. When Jesus therefore had seen his mother and the disciple standing whom he loved, he saith to his mother: Woman, behold thy son. After that, he saith to the disciple: Behold thy mother. And from that hour, the disciple took her to his own.

Day 9: John 21:1–14, 20–23

After this, Jesus showed himself again to the disciples at the sea of Tiberias. And he showed himself after this manner. There were together Simon Peter, and Thomas, who is called Didymus, and Nathanael, who was of Cana of Galilee, and the sons of Zebedee, and two others of his disciples. Simon Peter saith to them: I go a fishing. They say to him: We also come with thee. And they went forth, and entered into the ship: and that night they caught nothing. But when the morning was come, Jesus stood on the shore: yet the disciples knew not that it was Jesus. Jesus therefore said to them: Children, have you any meat? They answered him: No. He saith to them: Cast the net on the right side of the ship, and you shall find. They cast therefore; and now they were not able to draw it, for the multitude of fishes. That disciple therefore whom Jesus loved, said to Peter: It is the Lord. Simon Peter, when he heard that it was the Lord, girt his coat about him, (for he was naked,) and cast himself into the sea.... Peter turning about, saw that disciple whom Jesus loved following, who also leaned on his breast at supper, and said: Lord, who is he that shall betray thee? Him therefore when Peter had seen, he saith to Jesus: Lord, and what shall this man do? Jesus saith to him: So I will have him to remain till I come, what is it to thee? follow thou me. This saying therefore went abroad among the brethren, that that disciple should not die. And Jesus did not say to him: He should not die; but, So I will have him to remain till I come, what is it to thee?

When Jesus therefore had seen his mother and the disciple standing whom he loved, he saith to his mother: Woman, behold thy son. After that, he saith to the disciple: Behold thy mother.

Novena to St. John the Apostle

I

My most loving Saint, St. John the Apostle, behold me kneeling at thy feet, beseeching thee with all the affection of my heart to grant me thy special protection, particularly when in danger of offending God. O my dear and holy advocate, remember me before the throne of the most holy Trinity, and obtain for me from the infinite goodness of God, the virtues of humility, purity, obedience, and the grace to fulfill exactly the duties of my state.

(One Our Father, one Hail Mary, one Glory Be.)

II

O my dear Saint, St. John the Apostle, I renew to the Lord, through thee, the holy resolutions which I have frequently made of intending to love and serve Him faithfully. I am resolved to detach myself from every earthly thing, and I desire ardently to unite myself to Him, as my first beginning, last end, and sovereign good. My dear Saint, I beseech thee to offer to the most holy Trinity the sacrifice of my whole being, particularly of my judgment and will, in order to conform fully to God most holy, because I desire nothing else besides His grace and His holy love.

(One Our Father, one Hail Mary, one Glory Be.)

III

My sweet and holy Protector, St. John the Apostle, behold me again full of love for thee and full of confidence, beseeching thee to cast thyself on thy knees before the throne of the most holy Trinity, and entreat most ardently that God, through His infinite goodness, may grant me the grace to fly sin, and the gift of final perseverance. Thou knowest, O my dear St. John the Apostle, how great are the temptations to which man is subject, and how continual are the perils I run of being lost; do thou assist me with thy efficacious prayers.

(One Our Father, one Hail Mary, one Glory Be.)

Prayers to St. John

Indulgenced Prayer to St. John, the Apostle
O Glorious Apostle, who, on account of thy virginal purity, wast so beloved by Jesus as to deserve to lay thy head upon his divine breast, and to be left, in his place, as son to his most holy Mother; I beg thee to inflame me with a most ardent love towards Jesus and Mary. Obtain for me from our Lord that I, too, with a heart purified from earthly affections, may be made worthy to be ever united to Jesus as a faithful disciple, and to Mary as a devoted son, both here on earth and eternally in heaven. Amen.

Prayer for a Burning love for Jesus
O Glorious Apostle St. John, why for thy virginal purity was so beloved by Jesus as to merit to rest thy head upon His divine Bosom, and to be left, in His stead, as a son to His most holy Mother, I implore thee to set me on fire with a burning love for Jesus and Mary. Obtain for me, I pray this grace from our Lord, that, even now, with my heart set free from earthly affections, I may be made worthy to be forever united to Jesus as His faithful disciple and to Mary as her devoted child both here and on earth and then forever in heaven. Amen.

Prayer for an Ardent Love for Jesus and Mary
O Glorious Saint John, you were so loved by Jesus that you merited to rest your head upon his breast, and to be left in his place as a son to Mary. Obtain for us an ardent love for Jesus and Mary. Let me be united with them now on earth and forever after in heaven. Amen.

A Prayer for the Enlightenment of Saint John
Merciful Lord, we beseech Thee to cast They bright beams of light upon Thy Church, that it being enlightened by the doctrine of Thy blessed Apostle and Evangelist Saint John may so walk in the light of Thy truth, that it may at length attain to the light of everlasting life; through Jesus Christ our Lord. Amen.

A Prayer to St. John as Your Patron Saint
St. John, whom I have chosen as my special patron, pray for me that I, too, may one day glorify the Blessed Trinity in heaven. Obtain for me your lively faith, that I may consider all persons, things, and events in the light of almighty God. Pray, that I may be generous in making sacrifices of temporal things to promote my eternal interests, as you so wisely did. Set me on fire with a love for Jesus, that I may thirst for His sacraments and burn with zeal for the spread of His kingdom. By your powerful intercession, help me in the performance of my duties to God, myself and all the world. Win for me the virtue of purity and a great confidence in the Blessed Virgin. Protect me this day, and every day of my life. Keep me from mortal sin. Obtain for me the grace of a happy death. Amen.

A Parents' Prayer to St. John

St. John, chosen and favored disciple of our Lord, selected as the son of His sorrowful Mother, how great your privilege of being allowed to repose on the bosom of Jesus at the Last Supper, and to stand beneath the cross, there to receive Mary for your spiritual Mother! O happy disciple! How did you deserve such great prerogatives and favors? The whole Christian Church knows and acknowledges that it was your carefully guarded virginal purity which made you worthy of the special love of Jesus Christ; and that it was your ardent love and filial reverence toward His Blessed Mother that strengthened your heart to persevere to the end in the way of His holy cross.

O happy child of our dear Lady, how greatly I desire that my children and I may resemble you in purity of heart, in love for Jesus, and in devotion towards His Virgin Mother! In you do we place our trust. You will obtain for us this threefold grace. By your intercession you will dispose the Divine Mercy to pour out these graces into our hearts also. You are so highly favored by our Divine Master, He can refuse you nothing, least of all the graces He has so lavishly bestowed upon you. We confidently hope for these graces through your intercession, O chaste disciple of Jesus and devoted son of Mary! When you have obtained them for us, you must likewise watch over them, that we may never again lose them during our whole life. O pure St. John, obtain our request for the honor of Jesus and Mary and your own eternal praise! Amen.

Prayer to St. John for the Dying

Great Saint, who wast present at the Agony of Jesus, in the Garden of Olives, and upon the Cross, be present also at the agony of His members. Give this charitable assistance to all the dying, for whom I intercede this day, especially to those who have been recommended to our prayers. Intercede for them, and obtain for them, the grace of a holy death. O! beloved disciple of Jesus, ask the same favor for us, and for all dear to us. At the hour of our agony, be near us and protect us. Prepare us by a holy life, and by the imitation of thy virtues, for that great moment which shall decide our eternal destiny. Above all, obtain for us, a tender and real devotion to the Agonizing Heart of Jesus, and to the compassionate Heart of Mary, so that, having honored them on earth, we may love and praise them eternally with thee in Heaven. Amen.

And we know that
the Son of God is come.
And he hath given us
understanding that we
may know the true God
and may be in his true Son.
This is the true God
and life eternal.

1 John 5:20

Prayer Journal

Also Available from CatholicTreehouse.com

Saints

St. Anne	St. John Paul II	St. Michael the Archangel
St. Anthony of Padua	St. John the Baptist	St. Patrick
St. Benedict of Nursia	St. John the Evangelist	St. Paul
St. Catherine of Sienna	St. Joseph	St. Peter
St. Dominic	St. Luke the Evangelist	St. Thérèse of Lisieux
St. Frances Cabrini	St. Margaret of Castello	St. Thomas Aquinas
St. Francis of Assisi	St. Mark the Evangelist	St. Thomas the Apostle
St. Ignatius of Loyola	St. Matthew the Evangelist	... And more coming soon
St. Joan of Arc	St. Maximillian Kolbe	

Sacred Heart of Jesus

The Sacred Heart of Jesus Devotional & Journal has 125 pages of devotional prayers, hymns, and artwork that can help anyone develop their devotion to the Sacred Heart of Jesus, as well as 66 lined journal pages.

Blessed Virgin Mary

Honor the Blessed Virgin Mary on her five feasts with meditations, prayers, novenas, and classic hymns and artwork. Each feast is available separately, as well as one volume that celebrates all five feasts.

Made in United States
North Haven, CT
16 April 2022